GABRIEL MOULIN'S
SAN FRANCISCO PENINSULA

Town & Country Homes 1910-1930

from the
archives of
GABRIEL MOULIN STUDIOS
SAN FRANCISCO

For Jane C. Anthony,
Donna A. Parker and
Toni G. Ortonzo
　　　—Donald DeNevi

Project Designer: Linda W. Bonnett
Editor: Wayne Bonnett
Production: Ted Alexander
Copy Editing: Marian G. Witwer
Typography: Burch+McElroy, San Francisco
　　　　　　　Type by Design, San Rafael
Printing Coordination: Interprint, San Francisco
Printing: Toppan Printing Co., Ltd., Tokyo, Japan

Library of Congress Cataloging-in-Publication Data

Moulin, Gabriel, 1872-1945
　　　Gabriel Moulin's San Francisco Peninsula

　　　Includes index.
　　　1. Dwellings—California—San Francisco Peninsula—
Pictorial works. 2. Architecture, Domestic—California
—San Francisco Peninsula—Pictorial works. 3. Interior
decoration—California—San Francisco Peninsula—
Pictorial works. 4. San Francisco Peninsula (Calif.)—
Description and travel—Views. 5. San Francisco (Calif.)
—Buildings, structures, etc.—Pictorial works.
I. DeNevi, Don, 1937-. II. Moulin, Thomas, 1929-.
III. Title. IV. Title: San Francisco Peninsula.

F868.S156M68　1985　779′.4′0924　85-20236
ISBN 0-915269-01-5

Published by
WINDGATE PRESS
P.O. Box 1715 Sausalito, California 94966

FIRST EDITION

CONTENTS

FOREWORD

It could be said of Gabriel Moulin that he was the right photographer at the right place at the right time. Although he was acknowledged as a leading commercial photographer during the 1920s and 1930s, the historic value of his work is only now beginning to be recognized and fully appreciated. He was a skilled technician with a camera during the great age of mansion building in San Francisco and on the Peninsula. And, most importantly, he had access to the men whose names have become legend in San Francisco. His talents were in demand to produce photographic records of their homes, families and events.

The photographic technique he employed—exposure times of up to ten minutes, careful composition and focus with extreme depth of field—insured a wealth of detail in his studies. For us today, that sharply focused richness has a new value. We are permitted to browse leisurely through rooms and gardens that in many cases no longer exist. We can see antiques and furnishings not as museum displays, but as the owners originally lived with them.

The distinct images of Gabriel Moulin's photographs bring the early twentieth century on the Peninsula to life. To a historian, finding even one Moulin photograph related to a research project is like discovering a volume of primary documents. Seeing the one hundred and eighty exquisite photos presented here is like finding a treasure trove. They speak volumes about a way of life that is part of the fabric of San Francisco Bay Area history. They precisely designate the settings in minute detail, and they often portray persons who played vital roles in the life of the place. With the publication of this informative source, architectural historians will be able to interpret vintage subjects more accurately than before and to add to our cumulative knowledge of the period. What Downing's pattern books are to the Victorian era, this overview of Gabriel Moulin's photographic studies will be to the 1910s and 1920s. He who chances to open the book will find his interest aroused in Gabriel Moulin the photographer, and also in the period, places and people his art reveals.

Gabriel Moulin and other photographers of the era were often called upon to create photographic studies of private homes and gardens. Even after the introduction of George Eastman's handy Kodak, snapshots usually left much to be desired. Wealthy families who had spent hundreds of thousands, even millions, of gold-backed dollars on their homes did not hesitate to commission the best photographic talent available. Gabriel Moulin was in the forefront of a select group of San Francisco photographers. His log books read like a Who's Who of the San Francisco Bay area during the first decades of the century.

On completion of the photographic study, clients customarily received one enlargement of each choice photograph and one or more large leather-bound albums containing a collection of all photos taken for the series. Glass negatives and later film negatives were kept by the studio for a time in case additional prints were ordered. Eventually, if the client desired, the negatives were delivered to him. Many of the albums became treasured family possessions, passed on to new generations. But, unfortunately, many of the photographs were also lost or destroyed. During the 1960s, more and more vintage photographs began to appear at rummage sales and antique shops and as decor in restaurants and recreation rooms. Now collectors are recognizing the rarity and value of such photographs.

Fortunately, Gabriel Moulin Studios has preserved many of the glass plates and gelatin nitrate negatives from this era, and it is from this vast archive that *Gabriel Moulin's San Francisco Peninsula* was compiled. During the preparation of this volume, the publishers and the compilers Donald DeNevi and Thomas Moulin, grandson of Gabriel Moulin, determined to reproduce the photographs in their original size, with minimal cropping and retouching. In some cases when negatives no longer exist, original contact prints were used and no attempt was made to alter the effects of aging. Upon first viewing many of the photos one finds it difficult to believe they were taken over half a century ago. One shot of the Beresford Country Club in San Mateo (now the Peninsula Golf and Country Club), for example, looks as though it had been taken last week. On closer examination one notes Gabriel Moulin's 1912 Cadillac parked in the driveway. That, plus the treeless surroundings, reveals the true vintage of the photograph.

Moulin's classic photographs in this publication have benefited from modern technology. They are reproduced in two colors, black plus dark gray combined to accurately capture the full tonal range of the originals. This duotone process and the use of a recently developed laser scanner in making reproduction plates result in fidelity and crispness that would have pleased Gabriel Moulin.

Gabriel Moulin's San Francisco Peninsula does not attempt to fully describe San Francisco and Peninsula "Society" of the period, nor to illuminate the lives of all those who played a part in the birth and development of Peninsula towns. The plates herein represent some of the finest work of Gabriel Moulin: photographic images of a time past. Each photograph speaks eloquently of its time and place.

Dorothy F. Regnery
Portola Valley, 1985

Uplands

"The world went very well then."

J.D. Grant

GABRIEL MOULIN'S
SAN FRANCISCO PENINSULA

Town & Country Homes 1910-1930

compiled by
DONALD De NEVI & THOMAS MOULIN

project designed by
Linda Witwer Bonnett

WINDGATE PRESS
SAUSALITO, CALIFORNIA

Gabriel Moulin

INTRODUCTION

In 1924, Gabriel Moulin said about his photography, "I will never be one for the stylish soft forms we find in vogue today. My goal is to convert dry photo-documentation into a beautiful, clear, sensitive personal expression." And that is precisely what Gabriel Moulin did over the course of his sixty year career.

Moulin was schooled in the straightforward documentary style of photography that prevailed before the turn of the century. But, as exemplified by the photographs in this collection, Moulin's artistic abilities and technical skill added a timeless dimension to his work beyond that of many of his contemporaries.

Charles Peter Gabriel Moulin was born in San Jose, California, in 1872, the youngest of three children. His father Victor Michel Moulin was a French immigrant; his mother Caroline was of German descent. San Jose was barely more than a rural village when Gabriel was born, a farm community of several hundred inhabitants. The railroad from San Francisco had reached San Jose less than a decade before, yet the Peninsula had already felt its impact. Families, mainly wealthy beneficiaries of the Comstock Lode, were establishing large country estates and farms along the railroad route.

The Moulins went in the opposite direction, moving to San Francisco in 1880, where young Gabriel enrolled in Lincoln Grammar School near the family home at Fifth and Mission. Victor Moulin became a salesman, first of cigars and tobacco and later of wholesale fish and game. Gabriel's older brother Ferdinand got a job as a stock clerk, then was promoted to cashier for Cook, Ackerman & Cook. His mother was listed in early San Francisco business directories as a "teacher of languages, embroidery and fancy work."

When Gabriel graduated from Lincoln Grammar School he was twelve years old and ready to earn his share of the family income. By a stroke of good fortune he got a job as an assistant to Isaiah West Tabor, the City's leading commercial photographer, and so began his long association with photography. For the young apprentice, this was a golden opportunity. The craft of commercial photography was still relatively new, and most photographers were very secretive about their techniques. He was now assured access not only to a studio and all its secrets and fascinating equipment, but also to $5 a week in wages, a considerable sum in those days. During the years that followed, Moulin experimented with glass plate negatives in his off-hours, learning the methods employed by the pioneers of photography.

In 1891, when Gabriel was nineteen years old, he went to work for a year for photographer Max Karras. By the time of the 1894 California Midwinter International Exposition in San Francisco's Golden Gate Park, Gabriel had become an accomplished photographer, employed by R. J. Waters, proprietor of a large commerical photography studio in San Francisco. He was entrusted to cover the fair as a staff photographer for Waters, and he relished the opportunity to work with natural sunlight. From that point on, Gabriel Moulin was kept busy with outdoor assignments, a welcome change from studio work. His assignments were varied and challenging, taking him from the busy San Francisco waterfront to the serenity of the sand hills and to the fog-shrouded Golden Gate. During this era, San Francisco offered so many fascinating visual attractions that even lugging his heavy equipment over the hills and valleys did not dampen his enthusiasm.

Gabriel occupied his few leisure hours discussing art and photography with his associates and the young struggling artists of the City. During this time Moulin began his practice of exchanging photographic services for paintings and drawings by local artists who were short of cash. His friendships with artists and musicians and the growing recognition of his own artistic abilities led to an invitation to join San Francisco's Bohemian Club in 1898.

Gabriel Moulin soon discovered the tranquillity and overwhelming beauty of Bohemian Grove. Here, among the majestic conifers beside the Russian River, Moulin began a life-long love affair with the California Redwoods. He soon became the official photographer for the Bohemian Club, which provided many opportunities to practice and perfect his craft among the towering trees. His earliest photos of the Bohemian grove were made without benefit of modern filters and other sophisticated equipment. Although the shadowy forest was an elusive subject because of contrast between the shafts of sunlight and deep inky shadows, Moulin mastered it. His love of the California redwoods and his sensitive photography led to commissions from the Save-the-Redwoods-League. In later life Moulin was proud of the role

San Francisco earthquake and fire, 1906

Redwoods, Bohemian Grove, 1906

his work had played in establishing Redwood State Park, thus preserving some of the finest examples of California redwoods

In 1900 Gabriel Moulin married Christola Lena Morrill and in 1902 became the father of a daughter, Evelyn. The following year, Irving Victor was born, and in 1904 Raymond Morrill became the youngest member of the Moulin household.

At the same time his family was expanding, Gabriel became a partner in the R. J. Waters Studio. When the great earthquake and fire struck San Francisco on April 18, 1906, Gabriel rushed to the Ellis Street studio from his Broderick Street home and quickly gathered his camera and as many glass plates as he could carry. He struck out for the fire line as the conflagration swept the city. As he made dozens of dramatic photos of the devastation, the studio along with a priceless collection of glass negatives, was being consumed by the flames. Within hours the studio and the irreplaceable visual histories of San Francisco had been destroyed. However, Gabriel and the studio recovered from the loss, partly by selling his prints of the holocaust.

The dramatic events of 1906 helped establish Gabriel Moulin's reputation as a creative and meticulous craftsman. By 1909, he was financially secure enough to open his own studio on Kearny Street. Not only did earlier commercial clients seek him out, but Gabriel soon entered a new phase of his career.

After the turn of the century, the membership of the Bohemian Club included most of San Francisco's wealthy power-elite. Moulin's exquisite camera work was not lost on the likes of William Crocker and Claus Spreckels, who commissioned Moulin to make portraits of them and their families. Soon after, he was called upon to record elaborate parties at the homes of San Francisco socialites. As his reputation spread, he found himself in the palatial San Francisco mansions of luminaries of the time, photographing birthday parties, costume galas, debuts, weddings and even funerals.

In due course he was commissioned to follow the social set to their country homes in San Mateo County. Here Gabriel Moulin created some of his best photographs of formal gardens and interiors. His

Mark Hopkins residence, San Francisco, 1900

Millbrae, country estate of Darius Ogden Mills, 1895

assignments on the Peninsula also gave him ample opportunity to capture nearby scenes of almost unimaginable beauty; the Santa Clara Valley adorned with the blossoms of a million fruit trees and the simple country roads of San Mateo County, empty and lined with lofty Eucalyptus.

For Gabriel Moulin, San Francisco and "The Peninsula" were not separate places. Although San Francisco, situated on the northernmost tip of the San Francisco Peninsula often seems a world apart, it is nonetheless a peninsular city. Its only land connection is with the communities of San Mateo County, collectively known as "The Peninsula." Although for all Bay Area communities, San Francisco traditionally has been the hub of commercial activity, the bonds between "The City" and San Mateo County are deeper than those of mere commerce. In the days of the Gold Rush millionaires and the silver kings of the Comstock Lode, the wealthy and powerful nabobs of Montgomery Street acquired large land holdings south of San Francisco as the old Mexican land grants were dissected. The families that were the driving

force of San Francisco became the early "movers and shakers" of the small communities that evolved into Burlingame, Hillsborough, Atherton, San Mateo and other Peninsula towns. Slowly the populations of the small towns increased as the huge estates were broken into smaller parcels and new residents discovered the charm of Peninsula life. Towns that began in the 19th century as railroad stops to accommodate wealthy commuters became self-sustaining communities early in the 20th century. Still, their destinies were controlled by the small group of San Francisco families who maintained country estates there.

For Gabriel Moulin, commissioned to record the art and architecture of some of the most prominent families, the small towns were extensions of San Francisco society. Friendships and associations between Gabriel Moulin and many San Francisco and Peninsula families continued for decades, with Moulin recording births, marriages and deaths for two and sometimes three generations. In many cases it is an association that Gabriel Moulin Studios continues to this day.

Moulin's work then had also come to the attention of the best

Palace of Fine Arts, Panama Pacific International Exposition, 1915

Stanford University, 1917

known local architects of the age: Willis Polk, Arthur Brown, Jr., Bernard Maybeck and others. He photographed not only the sites for elaborate estates, but also the step-by-step construction of homes and commercial buildings.

By the spring of 1914, Gabriel Moulin was firmly established as a leader in commercial photography. Not only was his work comprehensive, but his compositions were so visually stunning that he was selected to serve as the official photographer of the Palace of Fine Art at the Panama Pacific International Exposition of 1915. After experimenting with the new Lumier color plates, he refined the three-negative process so well that thousands of the prints he made of the original art on exhibition were sold at the fair.

The 1920s were especially prosperous for Gabriel Moulin. The growth of industry, particularly shipping and its auxiliaries, was constantly bringing in new commissions. His son Irving joined the business in 1923 and Raymond followed in 1932. This expansion of his studio gave Gabriel more time for non-commerical pursuits.

Although he was best known as a commercial photographer, Gabriel Moulin was at heart a nature photographer. He meticulously and masterfully recorded thousands of offices, street scenes, weddings, home interiors and exteriors over his lengthy career. Yet during that span he also made countless magnificent photographs of nature at her finest; the redwoods, Yosemite and Lake Tahoe, Monterey and the open, uncrowded hills and valleys of Marin County, the Contra Costa and the San Francisco Peninsula.

The decade of the twenties saw Gabriel Moulin returning often to the Peninsula as a much sought-after "Society" photographer. In Hillsborough, then called the "City of Millionaires," and in neighboring Burlingame, Menlo Park and Atherton, it was very fashionable to have made a complete photo record of one's home. In addition to formal portraits of the owners and their families, Moulin applied his talents to gates, gardens, stables, garages with automobiles, carriage houses and of course interiors. He also photographed family summer homes at Lake Tahoe, Santa Cruz, and along the Russian River. When

Linden Towers, home of James Clair Flood, San Mateo, 1907

Baywood, home of John Parrott, San Mateo, 1911

children of Peninsula families established homes in the East Bay or Marin County, Gabriel Moulin was asked to photograph them as well. As Peninsula families expanded, Gabriel Moulin's Peninsula world also expanded.

It was in photographing home interiors that Gabriel Moulin's brilliance shone most brightly. Seemingly straightforward, his interior photographs are often masterpieces of meticulous planning, the result of careful composition, lenthy exposures and the use of skillful lighting techniques that ranged from natural light to magnesium flash powder to indirect electric lights. He avoided using props to enhance a room's appeal, although he did sometimes reposition artifacts within a room to improve a composition. Each plate recorded a direct honest image, filled with myriad details reflecting the owner's taste, or, in some cases, the lack of it.

Throughout the 1930s Gabriel Moulin and his sons were in the forefront of innovative commercial photography in San Francisco. Internationally, the studio was gaining a reputation for its pictorial

record of the growth and development of California industry. While his father continued to seek new ways of regulating the contrast of light and dark and developing negatives by varying exposures, Irving was pioneering the use of photography in retail advertising. By 1933, every major retail outlet in San Francisco using illustrated advertising employed the studio's line technique for conversion of their photographs. Raymond, meanwhile, continued to refine his recently designed aerial camera in order to photograph wider panoramic views of the city.

One of the studio's most cherished commissions was photographing the entire construction of both the Golden Gate and the San Francisco-Oakland Bay Bridges. Gabriel, then 61 years old, refused to accept the assignment as routine. Sensing the drama of men and steel, and appreciating the beauty created by the breathtaking lines of the mighty steel spans in different phases of completion, all three Moulins photographed some of the most dramatic work of their careers. While their father took the ground level views, the sons climbed aloft to

Andrew Welch residence, San Francisco, 1920

Percy Morgan residence, Los Altos Hills, 1920

shoot the more difficult—and more dangerous—panoramic scenes.

As the decade grew to a close, the studio received another prize commission: photographing the Golden Gate International Exposition on Treasure Island in 1939–40.

Gabriel Moulin died in 1945, leaving the studio in the capable hands of his sons. He had taught his sons, who in turn taught theirs, the craft of commercial photography. In 1957, Irving relinquished his interest in the studio to Raymond's eldest son Thomas, who had begun working in the family business as an apprentice in 1949. Since 1974, when his father Raymond retired, Thomas Moulin has carried on the family tradition of photographic excellence.

All of Gabriel Moulin's photographs have something in common regardless of subject matter. They all reflect his extraordinary sense of composition, his concern for clarity and the interplay of light and shadow. He never undertook an assignment that did not receive his complete attention, be it a studio portrait, a simple garden wedding or the construction of the Golden Gate Bridge.

In recent years Gabriel Moulin and his work have attracted the attention of collectors and connoisseurs of photography as fine art. As time erodes memories of the San Francisco Peninsula of the 1920s and 30s, Gabriel Moulin's photography takes on another dimension: documentation of an era. In time, it is perhaps this dimension of his work that makes the plates that follow an even more extraordinary collection. Although they are of an era now vanished, Gabriel Moulin's meticulous photographs permit us to contemplate what once was.

The plates in this volume are not meant to be a comprehensive study of the great houses of San Francisco and the Peninsula. They are, rather, representative of many town and country homes, some of which have been long since lost and some which fortunately have been preserved. The continuing efforts aimed at restoration and preservation of such grand country homes as Filoli and Villa Montalvo reflect the deep interest Bay Area residents have in their heritage. It is in the spirit of preservation of a small part of California's past that these photographs are presented.

THE PLATES

"Country homes are
comparatively numerous on the
Pacific Coast. This is largely
attributable to natural charm
and general habitability of
country. The proportion of well
designed country homes is large
when compared to other classes
of Pacific Coast architecture,
because country homes are usually
designed for cultured people by
architects who are similarly
endowed."

Louis Christian Mullgardt, 1915

1910~1930

PLATE 1 *Gates at Douglass Hall, Menlo Park, 1918*

PLATE 2   *Market Street, San Francisco, 1916*

PLATE 3 *El Camino Real, San Mateo County,* 1906

PLATE 4   *James Clair Flood's Linden Towers, 1911*

PLATE 5   *A Victorian interior*, 1912

PLATE 6   *The Augustus Taylor estate, Atherton, 1918*

PLATE 7   *Jacob B. Levison and family, Fair Oaks (Atherton),* 1909

PLATE 8   *Henry T. Scott's Oakhurst, Hillsborough, 1914*

PLATE 9   *Garden at Oakhurst,* 1914

PLATE 10 *The Carolands, Hillsborough, 1917*

PLATE 11 *The Carolands,* 1917

PLATE 12   *Dinner guests, 1928*

PLATE 13   *Writing desk,* 1925

PLATE 14   *Coal stove in The Carolands, 1917*

PLATE 15   *Sitting room detail,* 1927

PLATE 16   *Edward J. Tobin residence, Hillsborough, 1918*

PLATE 17 *Paul Fagan residence, Hillsborough, 1920*

EL CERRITO, SAN MATEO

Mr. & Mrs. Eugene J. de Sabla, Jr.

The site of El Cerrito was part of the homestead of William Davis Merry Howard, early settler of San Mateo County. Howard brought a small pre-fabricated cottage around Cape Horn from Boston around 1850. The wood frame structure was erected on a small promontory on Howard's *Rancho San Mateo,* called El Cerrito. Over the years the structure was enlarged and other buildings were added to the estate by subsequent members of the Howard family, and later owners including the Tobins and Walter S. Martin. Elaborate gardens were laid out and numerous specimen trees were established by John McLaren, who later became the renowned superintendent of Golden Gate Park.

In 1907 the property was acquired by Eugene J. de Sabla, Jr., one of the first men west of the Rockies to develop and market hydroelectric power and co-founder of the company that later became Pacific Gas and Electric. He retained architect Willis Polk to completely renovate the house. It emerged as the mansion shown here. Originally intended to be an English Tudor country home, the mansion was an interesting blend of English Renaissance, Jacobean and even a hint of the Carpenter Gothic lines of Howard's cottage. The original Howard cottage was not a part of de Sabla's mansion, however. Moved intact to a new location, it became in 1910 the first Burlingame town hall. In 1915 the Japanese tea garden from Japan's exhibit at the Panama Pacific International Exposition in San Francisco was moved in to the grounds of El Cerrito.

Eugene de Sabla and his family moved to New York in 1919 and sold El Cerrito. In the early 1920s the estate passed into the hands of Jean de St. Cyr, a flamboyant socialite. Throughout the next decade the mansion was the scene of many luminous events, with Hollywood celebrities and international socialites mixing with the local set. But the mansion was eventually sold as part of a divorce settlement and demolished in 1947. The Japanese garden remains, however, and the original entrance gate posts still stand on El Camino Real. The subdivided property today is the site of numerous homes, in both San Mateo and neighboring Hillsborough.

PLATE 18   *Main gate, El Cerrito, San Mateo, 1916*

Plate 19 *Approach to main house, El Cerrito, 1916*

PLATE 20   *El Cerrito, residence of Mr. & Mrs. Eugene J. de Sabla, Jr., 1916*

PLATE 21   *El Cerrito, 1916*

PLATE 22   *Entrance, El Cerrito, 1916*

Plate 23   *Main hall, El Cerrito, 1916*

PLATE 24   *Parlor, El Cerrito, 1916*

PLATE 25   *Sitting Room, El Cerrito, 1916*

PLATE 26   *Leontine de Sabla's bedroom, El Cerrito, 1916*

PLATE 27 *Japanese Tea Garden, El Cerrito, 1916*

PLATE 28   *El Cerrito, 1916*

PLATE 29 *Greenhouses and garden, El Cerrito, 1916*

PLATE 30 *Pool and bath house, El Cerrito, 1916*

PLATE 31   *Billiard room, El Cerrito, 1916*

PLATE 32   *Stables, El Cerrito, 1916*

1919 CALIFORNIA STREET
SAN FRANCISCO

Mr. & Mrs. M. H. de Young

In turn of the century San Francisco, a fashionable city address was a necessity for the socially eminent. Built in 1878, the 42-room mansion on "Outer California Street," was purchased in 1881 by M. H. de Young, co-founder of the *San Francisco Chronicle*. It soon became a San Francisco landmark address as the "General" and Mrs. de Young received and lavishly entertained potentates and luminaries from all over the world. Gala receptions were held for Theodore Roosevelt, the great Caruso, Ellen Terry, explorer Sir Henry Morton Stanley and the Crown Prince of Siam. Each of the four de Young daughters was presented to society at 1919 California Street, and three were married there. In the years that followed, M. H. de Young's granddaughters made their debuts in the old home. Two generations of children had played in the wide halls and the magnificent ballroom.

The interiors, as revealed by Gabriel Moulin's camera, were wonderfully eclectic. The Victorian era with all its genteel clutter was never more flamboyant than in San Francisco mansions. The self-made millionaires and power moguls of San Francisco's golden age expressed their fierce independence in the excesses of their homes. M. H. de Young's California Street mansion, although built by a previous owner, gradually became a reflection of his personality.

In the late 1920s, when Gabriel Moulin photographed the venerable de Young home, he knew the era of San Francisco's grand mansions was coming to an end. Like many of the old San Francisco families, the next generation of de Youngs established homes in Hillsborough and other Peninsula towns. Country homes, whether in San Mateo, Marin County or the East Bay offered rural amenities not possible in San Francisco. When Michael Harry de Young died in 1925, his four daughters were already married and residing down the Peninsula. In 1941, the old mansion passed from the hands of the de Young family and was demolished. Many of the paintings, antiques and furnishings had already found their way into the M. H. de Young Memorial Museum in San Francisco.

PLATE 33   *Downstairs sitting room, M.H. de Young residence, San Francisco, 1920*

PLATE 34 *Main hall, M.H. de Young residence, 1920*

PLATE 35 *Main hall, M.H. de Young residence, 1920*

PLATE 36   *Dining room, M.H. de Young residence, 1910*

PLATE 37 *Dining room, M.H. de Young residence, 1910*

Plate 38 *Display room, M.H. de Young residence, 1920*

PLATE 39   *Upstairs sitting room, M.H. de Young residence, 1920*

PLATE 40   *Sleeping chamber, M.H. de Young residence, 1920*

PLATE 41   *Bedroom of Charles de Young, San Francisco, 1920*

PLATE 42   *Bedroom of Mr. & Mrs. Michael H. de Young, San Francisco, 1920*

PLATE 43   *M.H. de Young residence, 1919 California Street, 1920*

ARNOLD GENTHE

Mr. & Mrs. Charles Templeton Crocker

When Charles Templeton Crocker, grandson of "Big Four" Charles Crocker of the Central Pacific Railroad, decided in 1912 to build a mansion in Hillsborough, he commissioned architect Willis Polk to create a 35,000-square-foot Neo-Renaissance Classic structure. His father, Charles F. Crocker, had purchased the 160-acre site, known as Uplands, in 1878. After his father died, Charles Templeton and his sister Jennie continued to live in the house with their maternal grandmother. Later, Charles Templeton Crocker acquired his sister's interest in the property and planned a new mansion as a wedding present for his wife.

The existing house was carefully lifted from its foundation and eased down the slope on skids and across the creek to a new foundation. The new mansion, a $1,600,000 project, rose on the site of the old house, with steel-reinforced concrete walls, handcarved marble fireplaces, and imported Italian, French and German interior detailing. Crocker went to Europe with his architect to personally select artifacts and furnishings. The war which broke out in 1914 as the mansion was under construction prevented the importation of marble and certain other handcrafted items that Crocker intended for his mansion. But in spite of the difficulties, he managed to create a magnificent structure that has proved durable.

Gabriel Moulin was commissioned by Willis Polk to photograph the construction of the mansion from ground-breaking in 1912 to completion in 1917. As the formal gardens matured and the mansion took on an established look, Moulin returned to take the pictures shown here. The Crockers were divorced shortly after completion of the house and it was occupied only occasionally after that. Crocker's interests took him elsewhere, but he kept Uplands in the family until 1942. The Crocker family again acquired the property in 1956, and with the assistance of Mrs. Jennie Crocker Henderson, the estate was then purchased by the Crystal Springs School. Today the mansion and a portion of the original acreage serve as a permanent campus for the Crystal Springs and Uplands School.

PLATE 44 *Uplands, Hillsborough, 1925*

PLATE 45   *View from the Porte Cochere, Uplands, 1923*

PLATE 46 *Uplands, 1928*

PLATE 47   *The courtyard, Uplands, 1925*

PLATE 48   *Formal garden, looking North, Uplands, 1923*

PLATE 49   *View from guest room, Uplands,* 1925

PLATE 50   *The pool at Uplands, 1917*

CLUB LIFE AND GOOD TIMES
Gabriel Moulin, Society Photographer

In the course of his assignments covering the social life of the Peninsula, Gabriel Moulin photographed country clubs, summer cabins at Lake Tahoe and Santa Cruz, yachts on San Francisco Bay, and countless events in the grand San Francisco hotels—the Fairmont, St. Francis, Mark Hopkins and the Palace. For Moulin, who preferred carefully composed scenes and lengthy exposures, the often candid shots of parties were not among his favorites. They are, however, enormously revealing and evocative of the era.

Country clubs, an American invention, provided meeting grounds where both men and women could enjoy sports like golf, fox hunting and polo that required more open land than most private estates provided. The clubhouse was a patrician version of the grange hall, serving as a meeting hall, dance pavilion and community center. The Burlingame Country Club, founded in 1893, was the first country club west of the Mississippi and the second in the United States; it was the nucleus around which the city of Hillsborough was formed.

If there was anything Peninsula families had in common shortly after the turn of the century, it was club life. The clubs, social, fraternal and service were part of the fabric of daily life. Membership in clubs like the Family and the Concordia and the Bohemiam Club provided a retreat for businessmen at a time in American life when men were expected to spend time "with the boys." Women also had their clubs, such as the Junior League and later the Women's City Club and numerous garden clubs. To be an active clubman or clubwoman was a social necessity.

Like many others, Gabriel Moulin found that club membership provided business as well as social contacts. For Moulin, the clubs and their activities were a constant source of photographic assignments, from weddings and parties to architectural studies. He was also on hand for numerous parties given in private homes by hostesses such as Alma Spreckels and Eleanor Martin. Alma, wife of sugar-heir Adolph Spreckels, was famous for her lavish and long-lasting parties in their princely Washington Street mansion in San Francisco. Gabriel Moulin was always on the guest list to record the festivities and the presence of the more and less famous celebrants.

PLATE 51   *Newhall Manor, Hillsborough, 1929*

PLATE 52   *George A. Pope residence, Hillsborough, 1915*

PLATE 53   *Burlingame Country Club, c. 1925*

PLATE 54   *Menlo Golf & Country Club, c. 1925*

PLATE 55   *Beresford Country Club, San Mateo,* 1914

PLATE 56   *William Crocker's New Place, 1920; the present Burlingame Country Club*

PLATE 57   *William Crocker's New Place, 1920*

PLATE 58 *Jack London and friends at Bohemian Grove, 1915*

PLATE 59   *Church in Portola Valley, built by The Family, 1910*

PLATE 60   *Bohemian Grove, William Crocker with "The Lost Angels," 1918*

PLATE 61   *The Bohemian Club, 1930*

PLATE 62   *Women's City Club of San Francisco, 1930*

PLATE 63 *Junior League Cruise Night, Hotel Mark Hopkins, c. 1930*

PLATE 64   *Clowns, Spreckels mansion, San Francisco, 1913*

PLATE 65 *Alma Spreckels (third from left), and guests, 1915*

PLATE 66   *Christmas party, Spreckels mansion, San Francisco, 1913*

PLATE 67   *Christmas party, Spreckels mansion, San Francisco, 1913*

PLATE 68   *New Year's Eve, Spreckels mansion, 1914*

PLATE 69   *"Pompeiian Room," Spreckels mansion, decorated for debut, 1930*

PLATE 70   *Dancers at debut, Spreckels mansion, 1930*

PLATE 71   *Entrance decorated for debut, Spreckels mansion, 1930*

PLATE 72   *Dance band at St. Francis Hotel, c. 1925*

PLATE 73 *Fairmont Hotel, decorated for wedding, 1928*

PLATE 74   *Hart-Bransten wedding, Old Orchard, Menlo Park, 1928*

PLATE 75   *Mr. and Mrs. Clarence R. Walter at Woodpecker Farm, Atherton, c. 1923*

PLATE 76   *Moore-Dillman wedding, Tres Ojos Rancho, Santa Cruz, 1928*

PLATE 77   *Moore-Dillman wedding, Tres Ojos Rancho, Santa Cruz, 1928*

PLATE 78   *Polo player, Menlo Park, 1928*

PLATE 79   *Mrs. William P. Roth with "My Joy," 1930*

PLATE 80   *Lake Tahoe, c.* 1918

PLATE 81   *Lake Tahoe cabin, c. 1920*

PLATE 82   *American saddle horse, Woodside, c. 1926*

PLATE 83   *Family home, Woodside, c.* 1912

Plate 84   *Children's birthday party, 1918*

PLATE 85   *Birthday cake for George Hadley, 1930*

2200 BROADWAY
SAN FRANCISCO

Mr. & Mrs. Joseph D. Grant

Joseph Donahoe Grant, son of a prosperous "forty-niner," became an industrial tycoon as well as a social activist. By 1908 he was president of the California-Oregon Power Company. Senator Leland Stanford appointed him at the age of thirty-five as a life trustee of Stanford University in 1893, and in later years Grant helped found the Save-The-Redwoods League. Gabriel Moulin became acquainted with Grant through their mutual interest in the redwoods and through the Bohemian Club. He was first commissioned by Grant in 1910 to photograph the stately family mansion on Broadway. The interior studies included here were made in 1915.

Grant was an aggressive sportsman with a love of the strenuous outdoor life advocated by Theodore Roosevelt. It was his athletic interest that first led him down the Peninsula where the Burlingame Country Club was established in 1893. He became an enthusiastic supporter of the fledgling club, helping to introduce both polo and golf to California.

In a canyon filled with native oak and laurel above the Country Club, Joseph Grant built a country home, a retreat referred to by his bachelor friends as a "shooting bungalow." When it burned in 1909, Joseph and his wife Edith Maclay Grant decided to build a larger residence on the site. Grant commissioned architect Lewis P. Hobart to design a stately Italian Renaissance residence on the Hillsborough property. The result was Villa Rose, photographed by Gabriel Moulin around 1915. At first the Grants used the Hillsborough mansion as a country house, preferring the town house on Broadway in San Francisco as their principle home. When Mr. and Mrs. Grant were traveling in summer, the children were delighted to stay at Villa Rose. Over time, the entire family came to love the soft rose colored villa and became permanent Hillsborough residents.

Both mansions survive today. The Broadway residence is part of the Convent of the Sacred Heart. Villa Rose, almost unchanged on the exterior and with all its original acreage intact, was renamed Strawberry Hill by a subsequent owner, and is today a private residence.

PLATE 86   *Joseph D. Grant residence, San Francisco,* 1915

PLATE 87   *Drawing room, Grant residence, San Francisco, 1915*

PLATE 88   *Drawing room, Grant residence, San Francisco, 1915*

PLATE 89   *Bedroom, Grant residence, San Francisco, 1915*

PLATE 90   *Bedroom, Grant residence, San Francisco, 1915*

PLATE 91   *Sitting room, Grant residence, San Francisco, 1915*

PLATE 92 *Villa Rose, Grant residence, Hillsborough, 1922*

VILLA MONTALVO, SARATOGA

Senator James Duval Phelan

Along with other artists, Gabriel Moulin was a frequent visitor to Villa Montalvo, James Phelan's magnificent country estate near Saratoga. In the 1920s Moulin recorded the following images of Senator Phelan's retreat on the hillside overlooking Santa Clara Valley. From its completion in 1915 until Phelan's death in 1930, Villa Montalvo was the setting for numerous dinner parties, receptions and special events. Prominent artists, writers and celebrities were invited to add color and substance to life at Montalvo.

James Duval Phelan, son of a Gold Rush land investor and banker, was the mayor of San Francisco from 1897 to 1902 and United States Senator from California from 1914 to 1920. A man of varied interests, he successfully combined skill in politics and a deep love of the arts. He was a lifelong bachelor, but hardly a social recluse. He embraced life with gusto and a fervor that was transmitted to those around him. His faith in California's future greatness and his love of its fabled past were the epitome of nineteenth-century Romanticism. Yet, in the setting of Villa Montalvo, it always seemed appropriate.

An invitation to pass the weekend at Montalvo in the company of Phelan and his coterie was a thing to treasure. Valued even more was to become a member of that "inner circle," comprised of a lucky few whose cultural contributions to California had caught Phelan's fancy. Good food, good companions, good conversation, music and poetry were standard fare at Montalvo. The natural beauty and serenity of the hills surrounding Villa Montalvo added immensely to the comfortable architecture of the villa and its gardens. This was life, at least in the eyes of James Phelan, as it was meant to be in a terrestrial paradise.

When Phelan died he bequeathed Villa Montalvo and the grounds to be maintained as a public facility, dedicated to the development of art, literature, music and architecture. Today the villa is a non-profit arts center under the trusteeship of the Montalvo Association.

PLATE 93   *Santa Clara Valley from Villa Montalvo, c.* 1920

PLATE 94   *Gateway to Villa Montalvo, Saratoga, c.* 1917

PLATE 95 *Lower Garden, Villa Montalvo, c. 1920*

PLATE 96   *Temple of Love, Lower Garden, Villa Montalvo, 1925*

PLATE 97 *Temple of Love, Villa Montalvo, 1925*

PLATE 98   *Loggia, Villa Montalvo, c. 1920*

PLATE 99   *Main entrance, Villa Montalvo, c.* 1920

PLATE 100   *Main hall, Villa Montalvo, 1924*

PLATE 101 *Main hall, Villa Montalvo, 1926*

PLATE 102   *Spanish court, Villa Montalvo, 1926*

PLATE 103   *Library, Villa Montalvo, 1926*

PLATE 104   *Pool at Villa Montalvo, 1926*

PLATE 105   *Garden Theatre, Villa Montalvo, 1926*

PLATE 106 *Luncheon, East Terrace, Villa Montalvo, 1926*

PLATE 107   *Lower Garden, Villa Montalvo, 1926*

PLATE 108   *Garden Theatre, Villa Montalvo, 1925*

PLATE 109　*Naval reception, Villa Montalvo, 1925*

PLATE 110   *Egyptian oblelisk, Villa Montalvo, 1930*

PLATE 111   *Belvedere, Villa Montalvo, 1924*

PLATE 112   *Josef Sigall in his Saratoga garden adjoining Villa Montalvo, 1926*

PLATE 113   *Saratoga studio of Josef Sigall, 1925*

PLATE 114   *Residence of Josef Sigall, Saratoga, 1925*

PLATE 115 *Residence of Josef Sigall, Saratoga, 1925*

ST. FRANCIS HOTEL
SAN FRANCISCO

Mr. & Mrs. Daniel Cowan Jackling

When copper magnate and widower Daniel Cowan Jackling married socially prominent Virginia Jolliffe in 1915, they celebrated their wedding supper in their luxury suite atop the St. Francis Hotel in San Francisco. A major financial figure, Jackling had a knack for acquiring fortunes and enjoying his wealth. In addition to his varied enterprises in metallurgy, oil, hotels, railroads and banks, he owned the *Cyprus,* then the largest private yacht on the Pacific Coast. Because of their extensive travels, the couple chose the St. Francis Hotel on Union Square as their San Francisco residence. His bride-to-be decorated the St. Francis suite, which occupied the entire top floor of the Post Street wing. The suite had a private elevator from Post Street and overlooked Union Square on the Powell Street side.

Daniel Jackling commissioned Gabriel Moulin to record his yacht and his extensive art collection around 1910. Shortly after the Jacklings moved into the St. Francis hotel, Moulin made these photos, which are the earliest known of the suite.

Eventually the Jacklings moved to the top floor and tower of the Hotel Mark Hopkins. Then in the late 1920s the Jacklings decided to settle down. They sold their private railroad car and yacht and gave up their hotel suites in New York and Paris. Daniel Jackling purchased a large site south of San Francisco and built a suitable country estate. The Woodside home, called "La Casita Espanol," was nestled in the oak-studded, gently rolling hills. A large barn and stables were on the estate for Daniel Jackling's newly acquired thoroughbreds. The George A. Popes acquired the St. Francis suite in 1929 after fire detroyed their San Francisco home. The Popes occupied the rooms for the rest of their lives. The name "Pope Suite" remained for three decades. The suite is now divided and known as the Dan London Suite and the City Club. Although the rooms were redecorated by the Popes, much of the original oak paneling and carved ceilings date from the Jackling era. The rooms were joined again temporarily when President and Mrs. Reagan hosted a State dinner in the suite for Queen Elizabeth II and Prince Philip during their 1983 visit to San Francisco.

PLATE 116   *St. Francis Hotel, San Francisco, c. 1915*

PLATE 117 *Hallway, Jackling Suite, c. 1917*

PLATE 118   *Drawing room, Jackling Suite, c. 1917*

PLATE 119   *Drawing room, Jackling Suite, c. 1917*

PLATE 120   *Jackling Suite, c. 1917*

PLATE 121   *Jackling Suite,* C. 1917

PLATE 122   *Jackling Suite with portrait of Virginia Jolliffe Jackling, c. 1917*

PLATE 123 *Library, Jackling Suite,* C. 1917

PLATE 124   *Dining room, Jackling Suite,* C. 1917

PLATE 125   *Deck of Jackling yacht*, Cyprus, 1915

PLATE 126   *Jackling residence, Woodside,* C. 1930

PLATE 127   *Virginia Allen at Jackling residence, Woodside, c. 1930*

PLATE 128   *Jackling residence, Woodside,* C. 1930

THE PINES, CLAREMONT
Mr. & Mrs. Philip E. Bowles

By the 1920s, Gabriel Moulin's photographic work on the Peninsula was well known. His reputation was so well established that children and grandchildren of old Peninsula families relied on his services. Moulin went wherever the occasion demanded. It was logical that his Peninsula "family" of clients extended far beyond the actual confines of the Peninsula. He photographed homes in Santa Barbara, Marin and Sonoma Counties and in many East Bay communities. Most of these assignments had their origins in long-established contacts made by Gabriel Moulin with Peninsula families.

Gabriel Moulin had a long association with the McNears going back to 1912, when he photographed the Atherton home of Frederick W. McNear. So when Amanda McNear Bowles, Frederick's sister, asked him to photograph The Pines in Claremont, Moulin was happy to oblige.

Philip E. Bowles, born in 1859, was raised in Santa Clara County and attended the University of California. In 1884, he married Amanda McNear, daughter of his early business associate George W. McNear of Atherton. By 1911 he was also president of the First National Bank of Oakland and First Trust Savings Bank of Oakland. Because of his business interests in the East Bay, the couple decided to make their home in the Claremont hills. On property purchased from the Livermore family near Broadway and College Avenue, they constructed a home around 1900.

Because Philip Bowles was an avid sportsman who enjoyed polo, golf and riding, and his wife was an active horsewoman and golfer, they followed closely the development of the Burlingame Country Club. Bowles, George McNear, Jr., and a few others formed Oakland Golf Club in 1898, on Adams Point near present Lakeside Park. The links were barely adequate and occasionally swamped, so the group looked for a more appropriate site. In 1903 the Claremont Country Club was launched and the following year property adjacent to Bowles estate was acquired by the club. In 1909 the Bowles retained architect L. B. Dutton to design The Pines, which was constructed on the site of their original Claremont home.

PLATE 129   *The Pines, Claremont, 1927*

PLATE 130   *Living room, The Pines, Claremont, 1927*

PLATE 131 *The Pines*, 1927

PLATE 132   *The Pines, 1927*

PLATE 133 *Entrance hall, The Pines, 1927*

PLATE 134   *Garden room, The Pines, 1927*

PLATE 135   *Amanda McNear Bowles in the Garden room, The Pines, 1927*

PLATE 136 *Sleeping porch, The Pines, 1927*

PLATE 137   *Amanda McNear Bowles in the greenhouse, The Pines, 1927*

PLATE 138 *Garden pool, The Pines, 1927*

PLATE 139   *Carriage house and garage, The Pines, 1927*

PLATE 140 *Stables at the Pines, 1927*

PLATE 141   *Amanda McNear Bowles in her Viceroy, The Pines, 1927*

FILOLI, WOODSIDE

Mr. & Mrs. William Bowers Bourn II

Mr. & Mrs. William P. Roth

Gabriel Moulin had a special passion for Filoli, the country home of Mr. and Mrs. William Bowers Bourn II, and later the home of Mr. and Mrs. William P. Roth. The elegant estate combined the architecture of Willis Polk at his best and the magnificent gardens of Bruce Porter and Isabella Worn. It was a place of quiet dignity, reflecting then as it does today, the pinnacle of country life. William Bourn had traveled extensively and spent considerable time in Britain. When he returned home to manage the family-owned Empire Gold Mine and the vineyard at St. Helena, he knew that someday he would have a large country house like those he had seen in the British Isles. It was not until after he had become president of the Spring Valley Water Company that his dream was fulfilled. On watershed lands at the south end of Crystal Lake, Bourn found the ideal site, reminiscent of his recently purchased Irish estate in County Kerry.

The architecture of Filoli is primarily Georgian, but with an eclecticism that reflects the individuality and taste of William Bourn. It was this sense of the unexpected when first viewing Filoli that appealed to Gabriel Moulin as a photographer. Moulin made countless photographs of Filoli, first for the Bourns, then for the Roths. He recorded the splendid interiors, the parties, and later even the Roths' thoroughbred horses.

But it was the garden at Filoli that captivated Moulin. He spent countless hours moving heavy camera equipment from one vantage point to another and studying the changing light in different seasons. He was inspired by the dramatic juxtaposition of brick garden walls, view corridors within the walls and beyond to the sweeping, open vistas. The plates shown here were taken in 1927 and show the garden in its original configuration and planting.

In 1975 Filoli was deeded by Mrs. Roth to the National Trust for Historic Preservation. Under the dedicated care of Mrs. Roth during her occupancy and the continued care of the non-profit Filoli Center, the formal garden is recognized today as one of the finest in the country. Filoli is open to the public by reservation.

PLATE 142   *Entrance to Filoli, Woodside, 1928*

PLATE 143   *The transverse hall, Filoli, 1928*

PLATE 144   *Library entrance, Filoli, 1928*

PLATE 145   *Drawing Room, Filoli, 1928*

PLATE 146 *Drawing Room, Filoli, 1928*

PLATE 147   *French Room, Filoli, 1928*

PLATE 148   *French Room, Filoli, 1928*

PLATE 149 *Library, Filoli, 1928*

PLATE 150 *Library, Filoli, 1928*

PLATE 151   *The Study, Filoli, 1928*

PLATE 152   *Dining Room, Filoli, 1928*

PLATE 153   *Main stairs, Filoli, 1928*

PLATE 154 *Upstairs drawing room, Filoli, 1928*

PLATE 155   *Ballroom, Filoli, 1928*

PLATE 156 *Ballroom, Filoli, 1928*

PLATE 157   *Center of the Walled Garden, Filoli, 1927*

PLATE 158   *Teahouse and Clock Tower of Carriage House, Filoli, 1927*

PLATE 159   *Teahouse from the West Terrace, Filoli, 1927*

PLATE 160 *South entrance to the Walled Garden, Filoli, 1927*

PLATE 161   *The Sunken Garden and Carriage House, Filoli, 1927*

PLATE 162   *The Sunken Garden, Filoli, 1927*

PLATE 163   *In the Walled Garden, Filoli, 1927*

PLATE 164 *The Carriage House, Filoli, 1927*

PLATE 165   *Mrs. William P. Roth at Why Worry Farm, 1930*

PLATE 166   *Why Worry Farm, Woodside, 1930*

PLATE 167   *San Francisco Peninsula, 1930*

PLATE 168   *Hillsborough, c.* 1930

PLATE 169   *Bride and bridesmaids, Old Orchard, Atherton, 1928*

PLATE 170   *Garden at Old Orchard, Atherton, 1928*

Praising what is lost
Makes the remembrance dear.

WILLIAM SHAKESPEARE
All's Well That Ends Well

PLATE 171   *Gabriel Moulin, self-portrait, 1928*

NOTES

THE PLATES

1. The gates at Douglass Hall served as an introductory statement about the mansion. Elaborate estate gates became almost an architectural symbol of early Hillsborough, "the City of Millionaires." Today, with many of the large estates subdivided, the gates are sometimes all that remain of the gardens and mansions they once protected.

In the case of Douglass Hall, the gates are gone, but the mansion remains. Built in 1906 by hardware manufacturer Theodore Payne and his wife Pauline O'Brien Payne, the 52 room mansion was purchased by Leon Forrest Douglass in 1921. Douglass, an electronics inventor and a founder of RCA, named the mansion Victoria Manor in honor of his wife, Victoria Adams Douglass. He also named one of his inventions after her: the Victrola. Today Douglass Hall is part of the Menlo School and College.

2. and 3. The appeal of country living is apparent in these two contrasting views: San Francisco's Market Street and El Camino Real in San Mateo County. Moulin's studio, like the businesses of many of his clients, was necessarily centered in the city. But the direct rail link between the City and the lower Peninsula made San Mateo County a haven for those who could afford both town and country homes, or for those who preferred to commute. The trend of building luxurious country homes continued until the first world war. In 1915, architect Electus Litchfield said, "The building of one's country house is a serious matter. The time was when for many people the town house was home and the country place more or less incidental, but nowadays the country house is home, while the city domicile is merely a temporary abiding place."

With the rapid improvement of roads and automobiles after 1910, more and more affluent San Francisco residents gave up their town homes and became permanent residents of new Peninsula cities such as Hillsborough, Menlo Park and Atherton.

4. Linden Towers was already a legendary Peninsula mansion when Gabriel Moulin first photographed it around 1900. Along with Thurlow Lodge in Menlo Park, Ralston Hall in Belmont and the Alvinza Hayward estate in San Mateo, Linden Towers represented the lavish show places, designed with ostentation in mind with a singular purpose to impress the owner's wealth and power on the beholder. Moulin, as a photographer, was challenged by the complexity of the structures and enjoyed the problems encountered in photographing them.

5. Moulin was fascinated by natural light in the often dark and gloomy Victorian interiors of mansions like Linden Towers. He experimented with drawn window shades and reflectors to control sunlight in his lengthy exposures. In this anonymous Victorian interior, he has succeeded in creating a light, almost cheery mood.

6. The Augustus Taylor estate in Atherton was another of Moulin's earlier assignments. This Greek revival home, designed by Walter Bliss of Bliss and Faville, was built in 1903.

7. When photographing country homes, Moulin preferred to portray the families in informal settings. Here, he captured Jacob and Alice Gerstle Levison with their children John, Robert, Charles and George on a quiet morning in 1909. Moulin photographed the Levisons' home in San Francisco and the Gerstle family home in San Rafael (which is today part of Gerstle Park).

Jacob Bertha Levison was a pioneer of the insurance industry in San Francisco, becoming a director of Fireman's Fund in 1906 and serving as president from 1917 to 1937. Following the devastating San Francisco earthquake and fire in 1906, Levison devised a plan of claim payment that saved the company from bankruptcy. In part this was due to his close association with the representatives of major claimants such as William H. Crocker, George A. Newhall and Henry T. Scott.

8. and 9. "Oakhurst," the home of Mr. and Mrs. Henry Tiffany Scott in Hillsborough, was built in 1898. Scott rose from shipping clerk with Union Iron Works in San Francisco to become its president in 1884. He became president of Pacific States Telephone and Telegraph Company in 1906, and by the time Gabriel Moulin took these photographs of his home, he was well known as a "captain of industry" with directorates in numerous San Francisco and Peninsula corporations. He was president of the Burlingame Land & Water Company and the St. Francis Hotel Company as well as of the Mercantile National Bank. Scott was as energetic in his leisure activities as he was in business. He was a founder of the Burlingame Country Club and a member of the McCloud Country Club and was active in countless community projects.

10. The ill-fated "Carolands" was intended as the home of Harriet Pullman and her husband Francis Carolan. An adaptation of Vaux-le-Vicomte near Paris, this Beaux-Arts chateau was begun in 1913, the year the federal income tax law was enacted, signalling the end of the mansion building era in America. Conceived as a definitive statement of luxury and grandeur, Carolands was to be on a scale considered sumptuous even by Hillsborough standards. Architects submitted plans for 130 rooms comprising approximately one million square feet. After reviewing several schematic plans, the Carolans awarded the commission to all three competing architects; Achilles Duchene and Ernest Sanson in France, and San Francisco's Willis Polk, who would prepare working drawings and supervise construction. Felix Passot was commissioned as interior designer to work with the architects.

By the time it was completed and the 500 acres of the original ridge top estate in Hillsborough were planned, the Carolans lost interest in the project. They were separated and never returned to the "Carolands." The extensive acreage was subdivided and sold, and in 1925, Harriet Pullman (who became Mrs. A.F. Schermerhorn) sold off the chateau and the remaining twenty-five acres. Spared from demolition, the chateau, with the grounds reduced to merely six acres, became the home of the Countess Lillian Remillard Dandini. After her death in 1973, the chateau passed through several owners until 1985, when the decision was made to demolish it.

12. to 15. When Gabriel Moulin was assigned to cover an event or document an interior, he was never content with just photographing the obvious. His creative instinct drew him to details others might have overlooked; a cluttered desk, an overworked stove, a fleeting expression on the face of a regal matron at a dinner party. It is at these moments that Moulin's photography reveals facets of daily life that museum exhibits of period furniture and costumes can never reproduce.

16. and 17. These photographs of the Edward J. Tobin and the Paul Fagan residences in Hillsborough represent the type of assignment most often given Gabriel Moulin in the 1920s. Composed to highlight certain architectural features, they became part of photographic portfolios designed to show an estate to best advantage. It was on the straightforward strength of just such photographs that Gabriel Moulin's reputation spread throughout the Peninsula and kept him in constant demand.

18. to 32. When Eugene Joly de Sabla, Jr. announced in 1907 that he would construct the finest and most expensive country home on the Pacific Coast, it created quite a stir. A descendant of French nobility, de Sabla was then forty-two years old and wealthy enough to give credibility to his claim. His grandfather was a railroad builder and one of the first planners of a canal across the Isthmus of Panama. Eugene was born in Panama on one of his father's plantations and came to California in 1870, where he became an assayer after finishing prep school. By 1890, after working in copper mines in Arizona and later for his father's shipping company, de Sabla had become involved in developing hydro-electric power and long distance electric power transmission to assist mining operations in the Sierras. In partnership with John Martin, de Sabla built power plants and consolidated utility systems that later became the foundation of Pacific Gas and Electric Company.

De Sabla's interest in the San Francisco Peninsula stemmed in part from his group's acquisition in 1904 of United Gas and Electric Company that provided power to much of San Mateo County. Impressed by the innovative applications of electric power for farm and industrial purposes on the Peninsula, like those on the estate of Walter S. Hobart and on Prince Poniatowski's Sky Farm, de Sabla decided that the Peninsula had a great future.

He purchased the thirty acre estate known as El Cerrito in San Mateo and set architect Willis Polk to work. Polk's original sketches show a Tudor mansion even more grand than the structure eventually built. The newspapers at the time claimed it would be "the first large country home constructed entirely of brick and stone." The advantage of building on an established site was that the fourteen landscaped acres of the estate were well matured and groomed. A contemporary newspaper said, "In the grounds at El Cerrito are, without question, the very finest trees of natural growth in California. Its oaks and bays are famous. In addition to this, the grounds contain the most magnificent specimen trees ever planted in California. These trees were all set out by John McLaren, the noted superintendent of Golden Gate Park."

When the thirty-five room mansion was completed in 1909, the de Sablas hosted the most lavish party, in monetary terms, ever seen on the Peninsula to that date. The occasion was the debut of their daughter Vera, and the tab for decorations, "refreshments," and reserving the entire Peninsula Hotel for guests was $16,500. Minute details of the "orchidean fantasy" were chronicled in the San Francisco newspapers, including a cost breakdown, a description of the original Paris gown and $15,000 bracelet worn by the debutante, and the colorful and brilliant lighting in El Cerrito's gardens.

The de Sablas sold El Cerrito in 1919 and moved to New York. The estate then passed into the hands of flamboyant socialite Jean de St. Cyr. Throughout the 1930s the mansion saw many luminous events, but it was eventually sold as part of a divorce settlement. In 1940 the furnishings of El Cerrito were sold at auction, an event that drew 6,000 curious people to view the sumptuous tapestries, rugs, furniture and objets d'art. The mansion was demolished in 1947. The Japanese garden remains, however, and the original entrance gate posts still stand on El Camino Real. The subdivided property today is the site of numerous Hillsborough homes. Gabriel Moulin's photographs remain as a testament to the splendors of de Sabla's *El Cerrito*.

33. The Louis XV and XVI style downstairs sitting room of the M.H. de Young mansion, known as the "Pink Room," was the scene of many receptions. With its ceiling murals and Mrs. de Young's fine collection of Dresden porcelain figures, this room was suitable for intimate ladies' teas, yet elegant enough to receive foreign dignitaries.

34. The main hall or "Blue Room" of 1919 California Street. On the blue tinted wall beneath the allegorical ceiling frescoes hangs a portrait of Kate de Young, *grande dame* of the household until her death in 1917.

35. Portraits on the walls of the "Blue Room" include those of two of the de Young children, Charles on the left, and Constance (later Mrs. Joseph O. Tobin). The room reflects a Victorian penchant for elegant clutter, and also serves, as did all the rooms at 1919 California Street, to display mementos of the de Young's wide travels. On the oak inlaid floor are Chinese and Turkish rugs, and period furniture acquired in England, France and Italy. The bookcase contains two large bound volumes of the collected letters of M.H. de Young.

36. and 37. The striking dining room at 1919 California Street was finished in antique oak with blue and gold heraldic figures above the sidewalls. The moorish arch leading to the alcove with its white marble fireplace was very stylish for the time.

38. At one end of the main hall, folding doors opened into the billiard room with its deep maroon marble Corinthian columns. M.H. de Young had little time for billiards and had the room converted into a display room, with built-in walnut cabinets for his collection of Chinese carvings. The story is told that in this room, while examining the exotic collectibles, famous African explorer Sir Henry Morton Stanley once declared he had never known the meaning of fear. At that precise moment an earthquake rumbled through San Francisco, and the intrepid explorer joined the rest of the group under the billiard table.

Always a collector, M.H. de Young once recalled his early "fad" for collecting things. "I do not know how I got the fad, but I began by collecting stuffed birds. I had more than 300 of them. Then in the course of time, I went to an auction and bought a large collection of Chinese carvings. I had to take the birds out to make room for the carvings . . . [Since] there was no room in my home for them, I had to put the birds up for auction . . . I did not want to dispose of them. I wanted to keep them. That is where I got the museum bug."

M.H. de Young, who with his brother Charles had founded the *Daily Morning Chronicle*, later renamed the *San Francisco Chronicle*, was always active in civic affairs. In 1889 he was California Commissioner to the Paris Exhibition and

served as a National Commissioner and vice president of the World's Columbian Exposition at Chicago in 1892. He became the driving force behind the California Midwinter International Exposition and was its Director General. After the fair in Golden Gate Park closed, the fine arts building was left standing to become a permanent memorial to the exhibition. De Young, long an advocate of a municipal museum for the citizens of San Francisco, proposed the name Memorial Museum (in memory of the Midwinter Fair) for the structure and began the process of gathering artifacts. For the remainder of his life, de Young was the principle and most enthusiastic patron of the museum. Today the M.H. de Young Memorial Museum contains thousands of objects collected by de Young, including many artifacts from 1919 California Street.

39. The upstairs sitting room at 1919 California Street was formal and more sedate than the downstairs "Pink Room." The wall on the right of the photograph bears the mark of a recently removed picture, a work of art very likely in the M.H. de Young Memorial Museum today.

40. to 43. Gabriel Moulin, who had first met M.H. de Young as a photographer at the 1894 Midwinter Fair, made these photographs of the bedrooms at 1919 California Street shortly after the death of the "General" in 1925.

44. to 50. Uplands, as designed by Willis Polk, contained 35,000 square feet of living space, with 39 rooms. By Hillsborough standards of the early twentieth century, Uplands was not immense. Yet with its beautifully groomed gardens and spectacular setting it was certainly one of the most impressive mansions built during that period. The interiors of beautifully proportioned rooms with fine woodcarving, matched marble walls and Italian ironwork make Uplands a Beaux-Arts masterpiece. World War I, which broke out in Europe as the mansion was under construction, forced some changes in the original concept. Instead of terra cotta as originally planned, the exterior is concrete. The exterior columns were also cast in concrete in place of Carrara marble. Fortunately much of the interior detailing from European sources had been shipped to this country before the outbreak of war.

One of the remarkable revelations about Gabriel Moulin's photographs of Uplands in the 1920s is how little development had taken place in surrounding Hillsborough.

51. "Newhall Manor", one of the first homes built in what would become Hillsborough, was one of five "cottages" designed by A. Page Brown and built in the 1890s by Francis Newlands, administrator of the vast Sharon estate. It was Newlands' plan to create an exclusive planned community, beginning with a cluster of fully developed homes. After a hundred or so homes had been built and sold, he would construct a country club to serve the residents of his community. He had successfully organized Chevy Chase near Washington D.C., laying out roads, water and sewerage systems, churches, schools and what would become the nation's first true "country club."

Sales were slow in his Peninsula venture, however, and a group of men eager for a club reversed the process. Striking a deal with Newlands, they converted one of the cottages into a clubhouse and planned a golf course and polo field, hoping to attract new members. The remaining cottages were sold and the country club was launched.

The first organizational meeting of the Burlingame Country Club was held September 1, 1893, in the San Francisco office of architect A. Page Brown. The first board selected at that meeting consisted of William Babcock, William H. Crocker, George Hall, J.B. Casserly, William H. Howard, Captain A.H. Payson, Harold Wheeler, John Parrott, Joseph O. Tobin, Richard M. Tobin, Hall McAllister and Major J.L. Rathbone.

George Newhall purchased this cottage in 1897, becoming the first occupant. It has subsequently been the home of S.F.B. Morse, founder of Del Monte Lodge, the Howard Spreckels, and in the 1970s, the Caspar Weinbergers.

52. The George A. Pope residence in Hillsborough was originally built in the 1870s by Alfred Poett and later acquired by William Sharon. It became the second home of the Burlingame Country Club in 1894 after being extensively remodeled by A. Page Brown to meet the needs of the club. In architectural style it closely resembled Brown's "cottages." It became the Popes' "country" home after 1899 when the club moved to larger quarters nearby.

George Pope was a lumber tycoon and son of "forty-niner" Andrew Jackson Pope, co-founder of the Pope Talbot Lumber Company in San Francisco. When George married Edith Taylor in 1894, the couple moved into a 35 room San Francisco townhouse on Pacific Avenue. In addition to the townhouse and their Hillsborough residence, the Popes maintained a summer place at Lake Tahoe called "Vatican Lodge." When their townhouse burned in 1929, the Popes moved into a suite on the top floor of the Post Street wing of the St. Francis Hotel, a suite once occupied by friends of the Popes, the Daniel Jacklings. Here the Popes remained the rest of their lives, neighbors of the other small but distinguished group of permanent hotel residents whose names included Magnin, Crocker, Fleish-hacker and Koshland.

Ironically, following the deaths of George and Edith Pope in the 1940s, their Hillsborough residence burned in 1946.

53. The fourth Burlingame Country Club was designed by Arthur Brown, Jr. and constructed in 1912. This clubhouse lasted until 1955, when the late William Crocker's New Place was acquired by the club. In 1927 the club considered purchasing the Carolands and its surrounding acreage as a new clubhouse, and in 1936 considered purchasing Filoli, near Woodside, for the same purpose.

55. Gabriel Moulin photographed the new building housing the Beresford Country Club shortly after the inaugural New Year's party in 1914. The club, incorporated in 1911 and built on land purchased from the Antoine Borel estate in San Mateo, had a prestigious list of charter members, including E.S. Heller, the first president, Walter Haas, I.W. Hellman, Jr., William Fries, Leon Guggenhime, Morris Meyerfield, George Roos, L.A. Schwabacher, S.C. Scheeline, Joseph Silverberg, M.J. Brandenstein, Joseph Sloss, Jesse Lilienthal, John Rothschild, L.W. Neustadter, Walter Stettheimer, Herbert Fleishhacker, Marcus Koshland, Albert Frank, and Albert and Alexis Ehrman. The original 18-hole golf course was laid out in 1911 and a small temporary clubhouse was dedicated on July 4th, 1912. Over the years the club has prospered, and although the site has remained the same, the golf course was redesigned in 1923. In 1946 the name was changed to Peninsula Golf and Country Club.

56. and 57. William H. Crocker was a capitalist and philanthropist in the original sense of the words. The youngest son of Charles Crocker, who with Leland Stanford, Colis Huntington and Mark Hopkins built the Central Pacific Railroad, William graduated with honors from Yale. Upon the death of his father and two older brothers, he assumed command of the Crocker business empire. By 1910 he held directorates in more corporations than any other California citizen and was president or vice president of fifteen banks, realty companies and assorted other corporations. He was a popular and distinguished member of nearly every social and service organization in San Francisco and the Peninsula. He had a deep interest in the Peninsula and despite his busy schedule was always available to advise fledgling enterprises, like the Burlingame Country Club.

William Crocker's "New Place" was built in 1906-07 in Hillsborough on the slope below where the Carolands would be situated. Gabriel Moulin captured the serenity and elegance of "New Place" long before it became the Burlingame Country Club. Designed by Lewis Hobart, the Second Renaissance Revival mansion was considered the epitome of how a family of the Crockers' stature should live. In 1954, "New Place" was purchased by the Burlingame Country Club and the following year became the fifth (and current) clubhouse.

58. Gabriel Moulin's long association with the Bohemian Club resulted in life-long friendships with many San Francisco artists and intellectuals as well as the power brokers of the day. He took hundreds of group photos of members and guests in Bohemian Grove. In this group in the summer of 1915 are:
Back row, left to right; Harry Leon Wilson, Pixley, Jack London, Edwin Markham and kneeling, George Ade.
Front row, left to right; Field, Gilbert Grosvenor, Dick Tully, George Sterling (on ground), Rufus Steele and an unidentified man. In the background watching the proceedings is Ernest Peixotto.

59. In 1902 a spin-off group from the Bohemian Club formed "The Family." Rumors and accusations that the Hearst newspapers were somehow responsible for the 1900 assassination of President William McKinley led to the expulsion from the Bohemian Club of fourteen members connected with Hearst's *San Francisco Examiner*. Others resigned in protest over the action, and the group formed the nucleus of the new club. The club, which was not to be called a club, but a "family," had a singular purpose: "To generate fellowship and fun by staging a perpetual round of entertainment and special events, directed, perfected and performed exclusively by members." Founding members included Henry J. Crocker, Sidney Coleman, Edwin R. Dimond, William B. Hopkins, Richard Hotaling, Jacob B. Levison, Ben Lilienthal and Joseph, Leon, Louis and Marcus Sloss. Animosity between the clubs was quickly forgotten and many members of the Bohemian Club also became members of The Family.

In 1908 The Family purchased a grove for their activities in Portola Valley near Woodside. It was here that Family members met Father George Lacombe, pastor of a little church near the club's trapshooting range. By mistake, some of the shot had been falling on the roof of the church and Father Lacombe was quick to inform The Family. After becoming fast friends with the Pastor (and relocating their trapshooting range), The Family decided to build a new, more substantial church. The result was Our Lady of the Wayside, completed in 1912. Much of the labor, materials and furnishings was donated by The Family members. Architect James Miller donated his services, and his twenty-year-old assistant Timothy Pflueger tackled the assignment with enthusiasm. Gabriel Moulin (a member of both The Family and the Bohemian Club), photographed the new church in 1913.

60. The annual summer encampments of the Bohemian Club, held in the club's redwood grove in Sonoma County, were very rustic in the early days. The Bohemians broke into small groups or "camps" within the Grove. Over the years, as the number of "camps" grew, they also became more civilized. Pitched tents on the forest floor gave way to permanent wooden platforms with striped canvas walls. Moulin recorded the changes in camp life, and the changes in membership. "The Lost Angels" camp in 1918 included: Seated, left to right; Judge F.M. Henshaw, John Gafney, W.C. Van Antwerp, Mr. Green, William H. Crocker, Carl Ahlstrom, J.D. Harvey, Sam Perkins, Dr. Ernest Bryant. Standing, from left to right; Mike Connell, Will Harbour, unidentified and J.D. Kingsley.

61 and **62.** Members of men's and women's clubs in San Francisco took great pride in the club quarters. Most clubs, however, rented space and as a result changed locations over the years. The Women's City Club for example has had six different locations in San Francisco.

The Women's City Club was founded in 1917 by the National League for Woman's Service of California, a group of public spirited citizens. The League has furnished volunteer aid during three wars, and in peacetime has been concerned with community projects, especially those involving women.

63. Gabriel Moulin photographed countless arrivals and departures of ocean liners during his career. This one was easier than most. Before the days of trans-oceanic air travel, the luxurious passenger ships of Pacific Mail Steamship Company and of the Matson, Robert Dollar, Oceanic and American President Lines were familiar to the San Francisco Peninsula social set.

64. Adolph and Alma Spreckels had not yet moved into their Washington Street mansion when Alma held the first of many parties in it. The identity of these clowns at her 1913 Christmas party is not known, but it is certain their number included well known representatives of San Francisco's business community.

65. Alma Spreckels (third from left) was known for her high spirits and bold sense of humor. The theme of her 1915 Christmas party was the "Living Doll." Here, Alma and her relatives and guests pose for Gabriel Moulin while keeping straight faces. Seated next to Alma is the gentleman who portrayed the "Living Doll."

66. and **67.** Alma Spreckels' 1913 Christmas party featured "Little Alma" and Adolph, Jr. as table decorations. Santa Claus is Samuel Shortridge, with Alma's mother Mathilde de Bretteville at his left.

When the children, with Little Alma in front, retired to the Christmas tree, Mr. Shortridge appeared without his false whiskers.

68. Alma Spreckels loved costume parties, and from the appearance of guests at her 1914 "Oriental Fantasy" New Year's Party, her enthusiasm was shared by others. Here the clowns, rajahs, storybook characters and at least two Kaiser Wilhelms enjoy oysters and champagne just before midnight.

69. to **71.** The debut of the Spreckels' daughter Dorothy in 1930 was the occasion for a party that lasted two days in the Washington Street mansion. The circular "Pompeiian Room" was often a focal point for celebrations and parties, and this event was no exception. Among other entertainers it featured the Heather Gordon Dance Ensemble, here performing on the east lawn. The east entrance of the mansion was canopied to keep out the San Francisco chill. Alma Spreckels' favorite holiday was Christmas, and she often combined the holiday season with other events, as in this case.

72. San Francisco's fashionable hotels in the 1920s were the settings for countless private parties. Dance bands were kept busy (as was Gabriel Moulin) with weddings, anniversaries, receptions, "bon voyage" parties and reunions.

73. Gabriel Moulin was often hired by San Francisco florist Albert O. Stein to record his elaborate floral arrangements for weddings and funerals. This photograph of flowers for the Dyer-Dunbar wedding in 1928 is an example of Stein's work.

74. Garden weddings on the Peninsula were as popular in the 1920s as they are now. Moulin was on hand for the wedding of Ellen Hart and Joseph M. Bransten in August, 1928. The setting was Old Orchard, the Atherton home of the bride's aunt, Mrs. Walter Stettheimer. The wedding party from left to right: Warren Hellman, Rosalie Walter, James D. Hart, Gertrude Lederman, Joseph Feigenbaum, Jean Stettheimer Warburg, Edward H. Heller, Elizabeth Mack, Martin Mitau, Ellen Hart, Joseph M. Bransten, Ruth Bransten Brown, Howard Ransahoff, Louise Rosenberg Bransten, Richard Bransten, William Bransten, Mary Anne Neustadter, A. Lincoln Brown, Nell Walter, Lloyd Dinkelspiel, Doris Weinber, Frederic J. Hellman.

75. Mr. and Mrs. Clarence R. Walter on their 25th wedding anniversary in 1923, at their Atherton home, Woodpecker Farm. Mr. Walter was a founder of the Menlo Circus Club and one of its most energetic supporters.

In 1920 a group of young girls from Atherton and Menlo Park, including Eleanor Weir, Evelyn Taylor and Katherine Doyle, decided to stage a charity circus using the talents of their ponies, dogs, cats and pet goats. From this first event, which raised $500 from ticket and lemonade sales, a tradition was born. The next year boys were invited to participate, and the circus was greatly expanded. By 1923 the Menlo Circus Club was formed and the performers played before an actual grandstand on a permanent site. The proceeds, by then over $2000 a year, went as usual to the Stanford Convalescent Home (now the Stanford Children's Hospital). Clarence Walter served as ringmaster for the circus for many years. Dressed in pink coat, white trousers and black boots, and cracking a long black whip, he became a familiar figure in the center ring. He not only drilled and rehearsed the young equestrians and clowns but saw to it that they put on a good show. Over the years, scores of Peninsula children have participated in the ever improving performances.

76. and **77.** Moulin went to Santa Cruz in September of 1928 for the wedding of Josephine Moore and Dean Dillman. The bride was the daughter of Mr. and Mrs. Charles C. Moore, and the ceremonies were held at their Santa Cruz estate, *Tres Ojos Rancho*. Moore, president of the 1915 Panama Pacific International Exposition in San Francisco, was a dynamic businessman who escaped to his 30 room country house as often as possible. The estate featured a private golf course, three lakes and a trout stream, numerous guest cottages, a dairy and complete riding stables. Over the years, *Tres Ojos Ranchos* was the setting for lavish parties with impressive guest lists, and quiet weekends with family friends and the Moores' grandchildren.

78. Horses have always been an integral part of Peninsula life. In the early days William Ralston would race the train with his matched thoroughbreds to Belmont, his country estate. In the 1870s Senator Milton Latham built a carriage house and stables at Thurlow Lodge, his Menlo Park estate, that rivaled many posh homes in size and luxury. When the Burlingame Country Club was formed, there was as much interest in equestrian sports as in golf. The San Mateo Polo Club was founded in 1912 and several local teams sprang up. The first match on El Cerrito Field was between the Whites, consisting of Paul Verier, Richard M. Tobin, Walter Hobart and Will Holloway, and the Reds: William Tevis, Jr., Thomas Driscoll, Edward E. Howard and George S. Garritt. Others who were early members of the informal Peninsula polo teams were George T. Cameron, Harry Hastings, Christian de Guigne, Jr., Francis J. Carolan, William Devereux, Joseph D. Grant, Robin Hayne, Elliott McAllister and Orville Pratt. Polo was popular on the Peninsula through the 1920s and 1930s until World War II. After the war, interest in the sport declined and the number of private polo fields diminished.

201

For women, there were equestrian events such as polo matches, gymkhanas and fox hunting. Skilled horsewomen like Mrs. William P. Roth and Amanda McNear Bowles received acclaim in the show ring and distinction in horse breeding circles.

80. and 81. Lake Tahoe was a favorite summer retreat long before winter sports became popular in California. After the turn of the century it became fashionable for affluent residents of San Francisco and other Peninsula cities to maintain cabins at Lake Tahoe or its environs. Even with the automobile, travel to Lake Tahoe was not an easy journey and maintenance of even a modest cabin was a luxury. Still, every August a number of Peninsula families made the trek, either to stay in one of the numerous lake resorts or in "cabins" that ranged from rustic to palatial.

The Tahoe estate of I. W. Hellmans, Pine Lodge, comprised over 2,000 acres with multiple boat houses and acres of lawns bordering the lake. The Robert Dollar estate was of equal size. George Newhall's Rubicon Bay summer home and George Whittell's "castle" were famous for their capacity for luxury. Elegant banquets with lavish food and drink, complete with all the refinements of The City, were standard. For others, Lake Tahoe was a retreat. With quiet rustic cabins where informality ruled, they escaped from the rigors of city life and the busy social schedule of the Peninsula.

Gabriel Moulin made hundreds of Lake Tahoe photographs and was a frequent guest at the summer homes of prominent Peninsula families. The photos shown here represent the Tahoe Moulin liked best: log cabins with huge stone fireplaces and a feeling of open hospitality, with easy access to the natural splendors of the lake and surrounding mountains.

82. and 83. Peninsula families were not always guests in other locales, but also hosts to those wishing to escape urban pressures. The rural quality of the Peninsula and the convenience of the railroad from San Francisco assured residents of a steady stream of visitors. Unmatched hospitality has always been the hallmark of Peninsula hosts and hostesses.

84. and 85. Gabriel Moulin photographed this birthday party in 1918 in a basement playroom of a large Peninsula home. Unfortunately, the identification of the children has been lost. Moulin also captured the moment at George Hadley's birthday party when the cake is about to make its dramatic entrance.

86. to 91. The Grant residence on Broadway in Pacific Heights was exemplary of the great San Francisco town houses. Formal and elegant, it represented wealth, permanence and status. Judging from these photos, however, it does not seem to reflect the outgoing, aggressive personality of Joseph Grant. Perhaps that is why he eventually came to prefer the life of a country squire on the Peninsula.

92. Villa Rose was a favorite subject of Gabriel Moulin's. When it was first completed he photographed it extensively for *Sunset Magazine* and *The Architectural Record*. Unfortunately, most of these photographs have not survived.

93. Villa Montalvo is surrounded by 175 hillside acres. Much of it in the 1920s was covered with cherry, apricot and prune trees, as was most of the Santa Clara Valley.

94. to 104. James Duval Phelan purchased the Santa Clara property for his country estate in 1911. He chose William Curlett, who had designed the Phelan Building in San Francisco, as his supervising architect. The concept for the villa was Phelan's, and although he was busy promoting the Panama Pacific International Exposition and promoting his own fortunes for a Senate race, he managed to find time to consult closely with Curlett. Construction began in 1912 and continued uninterrupted until William Curlett's death in January, 1914. Curlett's son Alex and their partner Charles E. Gottschalk took over the project.

Phelan was elected to the U.S. Senate in 1914 and took office in March, 1915, just as Villa Montalvo was completed. He named the villa in honor of Garcia Ordonez de Montalvo, a sixteenth century Spanish writer. In his novel *Las Sergas de Luy Esforzado Caballero Esplandian*, Montalvo describes an island called California, a lush paradise inhabited by Amazons. The legendary Queen Califia and her Amazons were transported about her realm by griffins, creatures with the bodies of lions and the heads and wings of eagles. The griffin theme is repeated throughout Villa Montalvo. Over the years, visitors to the villa presented Phelan with griffins in many forms, andirons, statuettes, paintings and bric-a-brac. A brace of griffins guard the entry gates to the estate, and griffins, sphinxes and other legendary beasts graced the gardens.

The main entrance (Plate 99), features heavy carved oak doors purchased by Phelan from a sixteenth century palace in Grenada, Spain. Above the doors is a large stained glass window depicting the *San Salvador*, flagship of Spanish explorer Juan Cabrillo. The main hall opens onto a small courtyard, with pool constructed on a terrace above the courtyard. A bronze plaque (Plate 104) contains an inscription composed by James Phelan. It reads "MDXXI Know Ordonez de Montalvo's Fame, Did He Not See, In Fantasy, Our California Grow, Out of Old Spain, Conferred Her Gold, A Paradise For Eager Eyes, His Dream Come True, For Me And You MCMXII."

105. September 18, 1926, was the second annual meeting of the Edwin Markham Society at Villa Montalvo. The Society was formed by the English Club of the San Jose Teachers' College and was a chapter of the Poetry Society of London. Gabriel Moulin was on hand for the presentation at Montalvo's Garden Theatre of poetry contest winners reading their works. The awards were presented by Gertrude Atherton. Honorary Chairman James Phelan is seated on the far right, and in the center is Chairman Dr. George Meade Bland, poet and close friend of Phelan and one of the organizers of the Society. Members and guests of the Edwin Markham Society were served luncheon on the east terrace of Montalvo (Plate 106), overlooking the Santa Clara Valley.

107. Following the presentation, guests were free to stroll through Montalvo's gardens. In this photo, two visitors at the sun dial in the lower garden are watched over by four Roman emperors, collected by Phelan during his European travels.

108. and 109. On April 9th, 1925, Senator Phelan held a reception for officers of the Pacific Fleet and their wives at Villa Montalvo. Here, Admiral Robert Koontz addresses the guests. Admiral Koontz, fellow officers and their wives (Plate 109) pose for Moulin at the entrance to a huge lawn tent, one of several Senator Phelan used for such occasions.

110. Senator Phelan's favorite dog, a German Shepherd named Boz, is buried near the Egyptian obelisk at Villa Montalvo.

111. It was perhaps this view of Villa Montalvo from the belvedere that inspired George Sterling to compose the lines that are most often associated with Villa Montalvo: "The hills go down to the east and the hills go up to the west, And here between bay and ocean is a place where men may rest; But the clouds and the winds they pass and the waters change and flow, And beauty, even when captive, seems ever about to go."

112. to 115. Josef Sigall, Senator Phelan's closest neighbor, purchased the 70 acre H. S. Kittredge estate adjoining Villa Montalvo in 1928. Sigall was a member of Phelan's "inner circle" and was eager to return the hospitality shown by Phelan. With his wife, the former Marie Stauffer, he transformed the estate into an artistic beauty spot, called at the time one of the most outstanding homes of Santa Clara Valley. Art treasures collected by Sigall during his extensive travels included sculptures and other artifacts which he placed in the garden and also tapestries, armor, swords paintings and sculptures that enriched the interior of the house.

A native of Poland, Josef de Sigall was born in 1892. He studied art in Munich and held degrees in law, science and philosophy. Sigall began a career as a portrait artist, painting many crowned heads of Europe, including Emperor Franz Josef of Austria. After being decorated by the Austro-Hungarian Empire during World War I, Sigall emigrated to the United States. He painted portraits of Presidents Coolidge and Hoover and members of their cabinets and scores of prominent persons, from the Vanderbilts to the president of Argentina. Senator Phelan, Helen Wills and Gertrude Atherton sat for Sigall, as did Phelan's dog Boz.

After a divorce and the death of Senator Phelan in 1930, Sigall moved to Los Angeles, where he painted portraits of Hollywood screen stars. In 1935 his Saratoga house and all its contents were destroyed by fire. Josef Sigall was so devastated by the loss that he never returned to the property. He sold it in 1945, and it was subdivided into several homesites.

116. Gabriel Moulin made this portrait of the St. Francis about the time the Jacklings moved into the top floor of the Post Street wing, seen on the right. At the far right of the photo is the Fitzhugh Building, and in the foreground is the Dewey Monument in Union Square, erected in 1903. Atop the monument is the figure of Victory, a bronze statue in the likeness of Alma de Bretteville, who posed for sculptor Robert Aitken. Alma de Bretteville later became Mrs. Adolph Speckels.

The St. Francis Hotel opened for business in 1904 and quickly became an important address for fashionable San Franciscans. Although heavily damaged in the 1906 earthquake, the St. Francis survived and prospered in the reconstructed city. The hotel was enlarged in 1910 and again in 1913 when the Post Street wing was added. One of the first residents of the new wing was Grover Magnin, who lived there for fifty-six years until his death. The era of residential suites ended in 1974 with the death of Edith Koshland, who had been a resident since the 1940s.

Throughout the 1920s, the St. Francis was a focal point for San Francisco and Peninsula society. Master chef Victor Hirtzler served up his creations nightly, and the White and Gold Room and the Mural Room (today called the Colonial Room) featured the big name dance bands of the era. It was also the setting for dress balls, weddings and other private functions. International notables and celebrities filled the guest book, and the phrase "Meet me under the clock," referring to the famous St. Francis lobby clock, was familiar to all San Franciscans.

117. to 122. The hallway leading from the private Post Street elevator was lined with part of the Jacklings' collection of fine paintings. The hallway opened into the drawing room overlooking Union Square. Featured in the drawing room were portraits of Daniel and Virginia Jolliffe Jackling. There were also paintings by C. T. Daubigny (Plate 118) and Corot (Plate 120).

123. and 124. Although the Jacklings had no children, their suite contained many photographs of the children of Mrs. Jacklings' six sisters. The library contained the same richness of pattern and elegant furnishings as the other rooms. The many leather bound volumes held the complete works of Voltaire, Thackeray, Scott and others. In the intimate, richly paneled dining room were displayed paintings by well known artists such as Thomas Gainsborough.

125. The Jacklings' yacht *Cyprus*, built in 1912, was manned by a crew of forty to fifty and had eleven staterooms with connecting baths. Accompanied by friends, the couple spent months at a time on the magnificent 231 foot yacht, travelling to all parts of the world. For land travel the Jacklings maintained a luxurious private railroad car, also named *Cyprus*.

126. to 128. For the Jacklings and the other permanent residents, the St. Francis was an ideal location in the heart of San Francisco. But even with the hotel's amenities, the Jacklings eventually longed for the serenity of country life. In the early 1920s the Jacklings moved to the top floor of the Hotel Mark Hopkins, but the yearning for open spaces won out. Jackling asked architect George Washington Smith to design a Spanish Colonial villa on his Woodside property. Smith, a master of that architectural style, responded with a magnificent home with a spectacular music room for Mrs. Jacklings' pipe organ. Plate 127 shows the Jacklings' niece, Virginia Allen at the pipe organ.

The interiors of the Jacklings' Spanish style estate in Woodside were a distinct departure from the St. Francis suite, although rare tapestries and fine paintings were still prominently displayed.

129. to 139. The Pines, Claremont home of Mrs. and Mrs. Philip E. Bowles, contained spectacular redwood interiors that, judging from the photographs, must have delighted Gabriel Moulin.

Although the approximately 150 acres comprising The Pines had many pine trees, the estate was best known for its flowers, in particular the Bowles' collection of Rhododendrons. Several greenhouses held hundreds of plants, and the house contained scores more. After the death of Philip Bowles in 1927, Mrs. Bowles presented the Rhododendron collection to Golden Gate Park in San Francisco in memory of her husband. The Pines also had an extensive rose garden, a Japanese Tea Garden, a large fruit orchard and numerous rare specimen trees. The grounds at The Pines also featured a stream that meandered through the gardens along controlled waterways and culminated in a pool near the center of the estate (Plate 138).

It is likely that Gabriel Moulin was asked to make some of these photos of The Pines following the fire that destroyed the nearby Claremont Country Club in 1927.

140. and 141. The Bowles loved fine horses and maintained a large stable of thoroughbreds. They participated in many Northern California horse shows for over thirty years. Mrs. Bowles sold The Pines after Mr. Bowles' death, and the acreage was broken into several parcels. The first subdivided parcel became "Claremont Pines" in 1929. The house and the last three remaining acres were sold in 1931.

142. to 156. A credo much admired by William Bourn was: Fight for a good cause, love your fellow man, live a good life. From this he selected the first two letters of the key words—FIght, LOve, LIfe—and formed the acronym FILOLI, which became the name for his country estate.

The main residence at Filoli gives the impression of an English country house except for its terra cotta roof. In the 1920s it was almost completely covered with ivy, which has now been removed. The house contains 43 rooms excluding baths, comprising 43,000 square feet. The main floor rooms have seventeen foot ceilings. The seventeen woodburning fireplaces represent many architectural styles, but of particular note are the ormulu decorated ballroom fireplace and the escallette marble dining room fireplace.

The ballroom forms one wing of Filoli's U-shaped plan, while the service and servants' area forms another. The principal rooms open from a transverse hallway that lies on the main axis of the house, parallel to the valley in which the house is sited. One of the main rooms, the study (Plate 151), features a portrait of William Bourn's mother, Sarah Chase Bourn (Mrs. William B. Bourn I). A smaller charcoal portrait done in 1915 by John Singer Sargent is of the Bourn's daughter, Maud Bourn Vincent. The two mounted Irish stag heads are from deer shot in 1910 at Bourn's Irish estate, Muckross, by his son-in-law Arthur Rose Vincent.

The French Room (Plates 147 and 148) is so called because of the fine collection of French mezzotints and etchings displayed there. The library (Plate 150) features portraits of Mrs. Bourn (Agnes Moody Bourn), and Mr. William B. Bourn II painted by Sir William Orpen. The magnificent ballroom at Filoli (Plates 155 and 156) contains crystal chandeliers said to have hung in the Hall of Mirrors at Versailles at the signing of the Treaty of Versailles. The murals in the ballroom are by Ernest Peixotto depicting Muckross House and Abbey and the Lakes of Killarney. The Bourns purchased the Muckross estate as a wedding present for their daughter in 1910.

157. to **164.** The sixteen acres of Filoli's gardens are laid out as several well-planned "rooms," separated from one another by brick walls. Originally designed by Bruce Porter and planted under the supervision of Isabella Worn, the formal gardens present a spectacular display in all seasons.

The Carriage House (Plate 161) was designed by Arthur Brown, Jr. Although it represents a departure architecturally from the main house, Brown's design complements the overall appearance of Filoli. The bell tower and clock of the Carriage House are patterned after a design by Sir Christopher Wren for Morden College in London. The Tea House (Plate 158), added to the garden in 1919, was also designed by Arthur Brown, Jr.

After the Bourns died in the 1930s, Filoli was purchased by Mr. and Mrs. William P. Roth. Under the stewardship of Lurline B. Roth, the gardens at Filoli were enhanced and continued to prosper. After Mrs. Roth deeded Filoli to the National Trust for Historic Preservation in 1975, the gardens and the house were leased to Filoli Center, a nonprofit organization that provides care and local administration for the estate. Friends of Filoli, originally part of Filoli Center, became a separate support group in 1978 to provide volunteer workers and fund raising programs for the benefit of Filoli.

165. and **166.** Always an avid horsewoman, Mrs. William P. Roth is shown with her trainer Lon Hayden at Why Worry Farm in Woodside, which the Roths owned prior to moving to Filoli.

167. One of many photographs taken by Gabriel Moulin on the San Francisco Peninsula.

168. This aerial photograph taken around 1930 shows Crystal Springs Lake (top) and the Carolands (upper right) with all its original acreage.

169. and **170.** Hart-Bransten wedding (see notes, Plate 74).

170. Gabriel Moulin made this photograph in an unidentified mansion after most of the furniture had been removed. For reasons known only to Gabriel Moulin, he set up the shot so that both camera and photographer were reflected in the mirror.

ACKNOWLEDGEMENTS

The publishers are grateful to all those who so graciously contributed their time and personal recollections during the preparation of this book. Because of them, the identity of many people and places in Gabriel Moulin's photographs will be preserved. We would like to express our appreciation to the following:

Mrs. E. G. Amark, Virginia Gill Anderson, Mrs. George Applegarth, Dr. Joseph Baird, Jr., Donald L. Blum, Dr. Mary Ellen Boyling, Alex Brammer, Mrs. Margaret Craig, Jerry Durham, Jack Dempsey, John W. Dinkelspeil, Larry Dinnean, Mitchell Postel, Mrs. Francis A. Martin, Jr., Mrs. Erick H. Low, Irving Moulin, Gladys Hansen, Mrs. Peggy Hart, Dr. Richard Loveland, Mrs. Thalia Lubin, Grace Hall, Dr. and Mrs. James Hart, Betty Horn, Mrs. Melita Oden, Hadley Osborn, Mrs. Barrie F. Regan, Millie Robbins, Mrs. William P. Roth, Gardner McCauley, Steven Powell, Bernice Sharlach, Dr. Albert Shumate, Dolly Toms, Mrs. Rita Thomsen, Timmy Gallagher, Lee Hunt Miller, Mrs. Walter Kuhn, John Rosekrans, Frances Moffat, Jean Wolff and special thanks to Marian Holmes.

We would also like to express our appreciation to the following organizations and institutions:

San Mateo Historical Association, Rare Books Room of the San Francisco Public Library, Filoli Center, Friends of Filoli, Montalvo Association, M. H. de Young Memorial Museum, Saratoga Historical Foundation, the Bancroft Library, Claremont Country Club, California Historical Society, Rolls Royce Club of America, Crystal Springs and Uplands School, Junior League of San Francisco, Women's City Club and the Stanford University Archives.

Linda and Wayne Bonnett
Windgate Press